WITHDRAWN

Introducción a los padres

We Both Read es la primera serie de libros diseñada para invitar a padres e hijos a compartir la lectura de un cuento, por turnos y en voz alta. Esta "lectura compartida" —que se ha desarrollado en conjunto con especialistas en primeras lecturas— invita a los padres a leer los textos más complejos en la página de la izquierda. Luego, les toca a los niños leer las páginas de la derecha, que contienen textos más sencillos, escritos específicamente para primeros lectores.

Leer en voz alta es una de las actividades más importantes que los padres comparten con sus hijos para ayudarlos a desarrollar la lectura. Sin embargo, *We Both Read* no es solo leerle *a* un niño, sino que les permite a los padres leer *con* el niño. *We Both Read* es más poderoso y efectivo porque combina dos elementos claves del aprendizaje: "demostración" (el padre lee) y "aplicación" (el niño lee). El resultado no es solo que el niño aprende a leer más rápido, ¡sino que ambos disfrutan y se enriquecen con esta experiencia!

Sería más útil si usted lee el libro completo y en voz alta la primera vez, y luego invita a su niño a participar en una segunda lectura. En algunos libros, las palabras más difíciles se presentan por primera vez en **negritas** en el texto del padre. Señalar o conversar sobre estas palabras ayudará a su niño a familiarizarse con estas y a ampliar su vocabulario. También notará que el ícono "lee el padre" 👓 precede el texto del padre y el ícono de "lee el niño" 👁 precede el texto del niño.

Lo invitamos a compartir y a relacionarse con su niño mientras leen el libro juntos. Si su hijo tiene dificultad, usted puede mencionar algunas cosas que lo ayuden. "Decir cada sonido" es bueno, pero puede que esto no funcione con todas las palabras. Los niños pueden hallar pistas en las palabras del cuento, en el contexto de las oraciones e incluso de las imágenes. Algunos cuentos incluyen patrones y rimas que los ayudarán. También le podría ser útil a su niño tocar las palabras con su dedo mientras leen para conectar mejor las palabras habladas con las palabras impresas.

¡Al compartir los libros de *We Both Read*, usted y su hijo vivirán juntos la fascinante aventura de la lectura! Es una manera divertida y fácil de animar y ayudar a su niño a leer —¡y una maravillosa manera de preparar a su niño para disfrutar de la lectura durante toda su vida!

WE BOTH READ®

WITHDRAWN

Parent's Introduction

We Both Read is the first series of books designed to invite parents and children to share the reading of a story by taking turns reading aloud. This "shared reading" innovation, which was developed with reading education specialists, invites parents to read the more complex text and storyline on the left-hand pages. Then children can be encouraged to read the right-hand pages, which feature less complex text and storyline, specifically written for the beginning reader.

Reading aloud is one of the most important activities parents can share with their child to assist in his or her reading development. However, *We Both Read* goes beyond reading *to* a child and allows parents to share the reading *with* a child. *We Both Read* is so powerful and effective because it combines two key elements in learning: "modeling" (the parent reads) and "doing" (the child reads). The result is not only faster reading development for the child but a much more enjoyable and enriching experience for both!

You may find it helpful to read the entire book aloud yourself the first time, then invite your child to participate in the second reading. In some books, a few more difficult words will first be introduced in the parent's text, distinguished with **bold lettering**. Pointing out, and even discussing, these words will help familiarize your child with them and help to build your child's vocabulary. Also, note that a "talking parent" icon ⚪ precedes the parent's text and a "talking child" icon ⚪ precedes the child's text.

We encourage you to share and interact with your child as you read the book together. If your child is having difficulty, you might want to mention a few things to help him or her. "Sounding out" is good, but it will not work with all words. Children can pick up clues about the words they are reading from the story, the context of the sentence, or even the pictures. Some stories have rhyming patterns that might help. It might also help them to touch the words with their finger as they read, to better connect the spoken words and the printed words.

Sharing the *We Both Read* books together will engage you and your child in an interactive adventure in reading! It is a fun and easy way to encourage and help your child to read—and a wonderful way to start your child off on a lifetime of reading enjoyment!

We All Sleep
Todos dormimos
A We Both Read® Book

For my sweet-pea, Natalie
D. J. P.

To Nicole, Colin, Roxanne & Kiko—the best kids ever!
G. L.

Text Copyright © 2009 by D. J. Panec
Illustrations Copyright © 2009 by Gloria Lapuyade
Editorial and Production Services by Cambridge BrickHouse, Inc.
Spanish translation © 2014 by Treasure Bay, Inc.
All rights reserved

We Both Read® is a trademark of Treasure Bay, Inc.

Published by Treasure Bay, Inc.
P.O. Box 119
Novato, CA 94948 USA

Printed in Singapore

Library of Congress Catalog Card Number: 2013930839

Paperback ISBN: 978-1-60115-054-7

We Both Read® Books
Patent No. 5,957,693

Visit us online at:
www.WeBothRead.com

PR 11-13

WE BOTH READ®

We All Sleep
Todos dormimos

By D. J. Panec

Translated by Yanitzia Canetti

Illustrated by Gloria Lapuyade

TREASURE BAY

In hopes they will spy a small worm from the sky,
the birds are all flying and soaring up **high.**
Are the birds flying down low?
No, the birds are flying up . . .

*Con la esperanza de hallar un gusanito desde el cielo,
todos los pájaros van hacia arriba; **elevan** el vuelo.
¿Bajan los pájaros volando?
No, ¡ellos se están . . .*

. . . high!

. . . elevando!

The sun disappears as it sets in the west.
It's time for some **sleep**. We need to rest.
For people and animals, **sleep** is the key.
The birds **sleep** in their big nest in the tree.
Shhh! The birds are . . .

Poniéndose por el oeste, el sol se empieza a ocultar.
*Es hora de **dormir**. Necesitamos descansar.*
*Para la gente y los animales, **dormir** es fundamental*
*Las aves pueden **dormir** en un nido colosal.*
¡Shhh! ¡Las aves están . . .

. . . sleeping!

. . . durmiendo!

They roll in the **dirt**, they're playing all day.
These pigs were once pinkish, but now they're more
gray. Are these pigs clean?

*Se revuelcan en el **lodo**, se pasan el día jugando.
Una vez fueron rosados, pero hacia el gris van
cambiando. ¿Están limpios estos cerditos?*

 No, they are a
little bit **dirty**!

*¡No, aún tienen **lodo**!*
¡Solo un poquito!

They are so dirty and really a sight!
I just hope they bathe before bedtime tonight!
Do you think he washed there, in back of his ear?
They're **sleeping** right now, so let's not get too near.

¡Están tan sucios que son dignos de admirar!
¡Espero que estén bañados antes de irse a acostar!
¿Crees que se lavaron bien detrás de las orejitas?
*Ya están **durmiendo**, no pases tan cerquita.*

Shhh! The pigs
are **sleeping**!

*¡Shhh! ¡Los cerditos
están **durmiendo**!*

The cubs that are wrestling are so very **small**.
But soon they will grow into bears that are tall.
Are the bear cubs big?

Los ositos que luchan son **pequeños** todavía.
Pero en enormes osos se convertirán un día.
¿Son grandes los ositos?

No, the bear cubs are **small**!

*¡No, los ositos son **pequeños**!*

 The **bears** like to hibernate all winter long.
To wake them up early would surely be wrong.
Come spring they will rise and find something to eat.
Perhaps now they're dreaming of honey, so sweet.

*Durante el largo invierno, a los **osos** les gusta hibernar.*
Despertarlos temprano, sería un error sin par.
Al llegar la primavera, salen a buscar comida.
Quizás sueñan con la miel, lo más dulce de la vida.

Shhh! The **bears** are sleeping!

*¡Shhh! ¡Los **osos** están durmiendo!*

These kittens are curious! Look how they try,
to catch anything that is **fast** or that flies.
Are the kittens slow?

¡Qué curiosos los gatitos! Mira cómo están tratando
de atrapar algo *veloz* o que esté volando.
¿Son lentos los gatitos?

No, they are **fast**!

*¡No, ellos son **veloces**!*

I don't think the **kittens** will catch that quick mouse.
Let's hope as they chase, they do not wreck the house!
Oh, look at them now, they are lying in the sun!
A short little nap, before having more fun.

*No creo que los **gatitos** atrapen al veloz ratón.*
¡Ojalá no destruyan la casa en la persecución!
¡Ah, míralos ahora, están echados al sol!
Una breve siestita, antes de tener más diversión.

Shhh! The **kittens** are sleeping!

*¡Shhh! ¡Los **gatitos** están durmiendo!*

These penguins all live in a place that is **cold**.
It always snows and it's icy all year, I am told.
Are the penguins hot?

*Estos pingüinos viven todos en un **frío** lugar.*
Donde el año entero hay hielo y nieva sin parar.
Estos pingüinos, ¿tienen calor?

No, they are **cold**!

*¡No, ellos tienen **frío**!*

The **penguins** will slide on the snow and then dive.
They swim like the fish, which they eat to survive.
On the ice, they will huddle in groups to stay warm.
With clouds in the sky, they all know it might storm.

*Los **pingüinos** se van a deslizar y luego a zambullir.*
Nadan como los peces; se los comen para sobrevivir.
Se amontonan para mantenerse calientes sobre el hielo.
Saben que habrá tormenta si hay nubes en el cielo.

Shhh! The **penguins** are sleeping!

*¡Shhh! Los **pingüinos** están durmiendo!*

The legs on a rabbit can help it to hop.
They land with a thump, as their **long** ears go flop.
Are the rabbit's ears short?

Las patas del conejo pueden ayudarlo a saltar.
*Estas retumban y sus **largas** orejas caen al aterrizar.*
¿Son cortas las orejas del conejo?

No, the rabbit's ears are **long**.

*No, las orejas del conejo son **largas**.*

Some **rabbits** are pets and some others are wild.
The one with the itch, I am sure he just smiled.
They sleep in their burrows, deep under the ground.
So no one will hear them, they make not a sound.

*Algunos **conejos** son salvajes y otros domésticos.*
Yo creo que solo sonríe el que tiene picazón.
En lo profundo del suelo, duermen en madrigueras.
Allí nadie los escucha, no hacen un ruido siquiera.

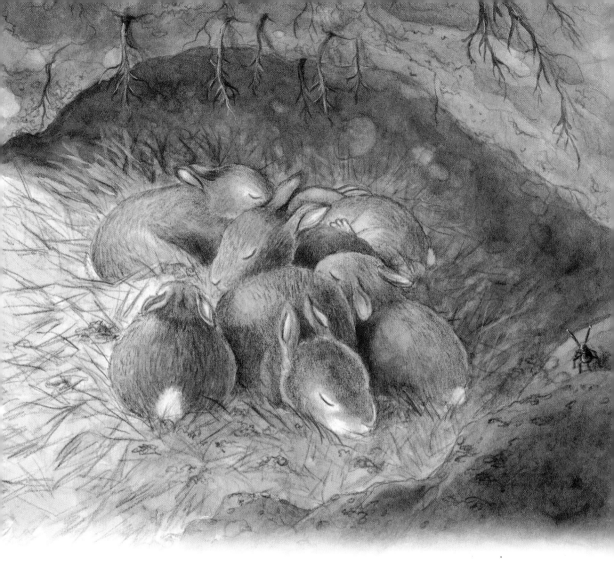

Shhh! The **rabbits** are sleeping!

*¡Shhh! Los **conejos** están durmiendo!*

Most puppies are friendly and love to play tug,
To make them feel **happy,** just give them a hug!
Are these puppies sad?

Los perritos son amistosos y así les encanta jugar.
*Para ponerlos **contentos,** ¡solo los tienes que abrazar!*
¿Están tristes estos perritos?

No, these puppies are happy!

*¡No, estos perritos están **contentos**!*

They'll jump and they'll yelp and they'll run 'til they drop.
I'm not sure they'll hear, if you ask them to stop.
But when the sun sets, little **puppies** will yawn.
Just watch as they curl up and doze until dawn.

Van a saltar, van aullar y a correr hasta caerse.
Seguro no te harán caso si les pides detenerse.
*Pero al ponerse el sol, bostezarán los **perritos**.*
Dormirán hasta el amanecer, mira qué acurrucaditos.

Shhh! The **puppies** are sleeping!

*¡Shhh! Los **perritos** están durmiendo!*

The bats like to sleep in the daytime, I've heard,
and wake up at **night**, when they fly like a bird.
Do bats fly during the day?

A los murciélagos les gusta dormir de día, se sabe.
*Y despiertan de **noche** para volar como un ave.*
¿Vuelan de día los murciélagos?

No, bats fly during the **night**.

*No, los murciélagos vuelan de **noche**.*

They eat hoards of insects. This helps us a lot,
since too many bugs are too many to swat!
Their feeding's all done; now the **bats** fly back home.
They'll sleep upside down in a deep cavern's dome.

Comen hordas de insectos. ¡Nos logran ayudar!
¡Pues tantos insectos, son muchos para aplastar!
*Al terminar de comer, los **murciélagos** a casa volarán.*
Y en el techo de una cueva, de cabeza dormirán.

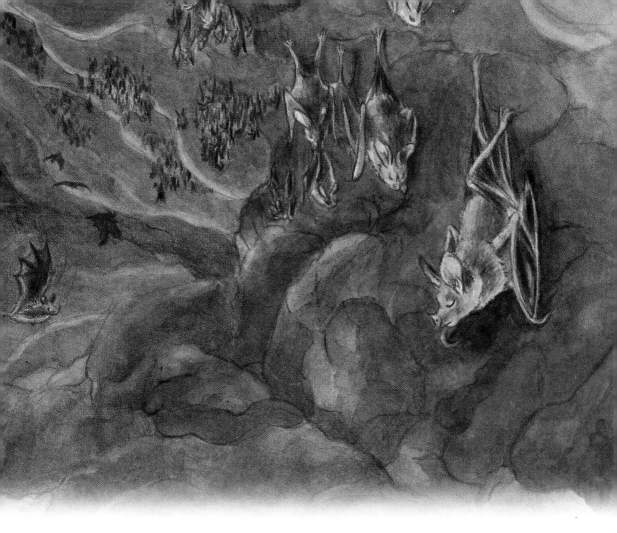

Shhh! The **bats** are sleeping!

*¡Shhh! Los **murciélagos** están durmiendo!*

The baby tries walking, then falls in the dirt.
His cry is so **loud** that my ears start to hurt!
Is this baby quiet?

El bebé se cae al suelo al tratar de caminar.
*¡Su llanto es tan **ruidoso** que mis oídos van a estallar!*
Este bebé, ¿es silencioso?

No, he is **loud**!

*¡No, es **ruidoso**!*

The **baby** makes sounds, but he can't talk.
He takes little steps as he's learning to walk.
But now he is tired and lies in my lap.
Let's be very quiet and just let him nap.

*El **bebé** hace sonidos, pero no puede hablar.*
Él da pasitos mientras aprende a caminar.
Pero ya está cansado y en mi regazo se recuesta.
Vamos a hacer silencio para que tome una siesta.

Shhh! The **baby** is sleeping.

*¡Shhh! El **bebé** está durmiendo.*

You make it seem **easy**! You're reading so fine!
Yes, soon you will read all of your part and mine.
Is reading this book hard?

*¡Logras que parezca **fácil**! ¡Estás leyendo muy bien!*
Sí, pronto leerás toda tu parte y la mía también.
¿Es difícil leer este libro?

No, reading this book is **easy**!

*¡No, leer este libro es **fácil**!*

We're both a bit tired, my friend, I agree,
but **I am** so glad you have read this with me.
Your eyes are so droopy, it's hard to ignore.
In one minute more, you'll be starting to snore!

Los dos estamos un poquito cansados, amigo,
*pero qué feliz **estoy de** que hayas leído conmigo.*
Tus ojos están caídos, es difícil de ignorar.
En un minuto más, ¡empezarás a roncar!

Shhh! **I am** sleeping.

*¡Shhh! **Estoy** durmiendo.*

If you liked **We All Sleep,** here is another
We Both Read® Book you are sure to enjoy!

*Si te gustó leer **Todos dormimos,** ¡seguramente disfrutarás
al leer este otro libro de la serie We Both Read®!*

Learn interesting information about the
world's most popular pet, including some of
the special ways dogs help and serve us.

*Aprende cosas interesantes sobre la mascota
más popular del mundo, incluso las formas
especiales en que los perros nos ayudan y nos
sirven.*

To see all the We Both Read® books that are available,
just go online to **www.WeBothRead.com**

*Para ver todos los libros disponibles de la serie We Both Read®,
visita nuestra página web: **www.WeBothRead.com***